SABRINA FISHER REECE

Depression Is Not the Boss of Me

I'm Snatching Back My Life

In59Seconds Publishing Co

First published by In59Seconds Publishing 2026

First edition

This book was professionally typeset on Reedsy.
Find out more at reedsy.com

I know what it feels like to be depressed. I know how heavy, isolating, and debilitating it can be. Some days, just getting through the day feels like a victory. But please don't give up. Depression does not get the final word. There is light ahead, even if you can't see it yet. Brighter days do come. Healing is possible, and your life is still worth fighting for. I Love You
-Bri Reece

Contents

Preface

This book was not written because I had all the answers. It was written because I've been in the fight. If you're holding this book, chances are you're tired. Not just physically tired—but tired in a way sleep doesn't fix. Tired of pushing through. Tired of pretending you're okay. Tired of feeling like depression has been calling the shots in your life while you quietly try to survive another day. I know that place well.

Depression doesn't always arrive dramatically. Sometimes it settles in slowly, over years. Sometimes it grows out of grief, abandonment, trauma, disappointment, or exhaustion. Sometimes it shows up when you've been strong for too long without support. And sometimes it doesn't come from one thing at all, it comes from life piling on until your spirit starts to feel heavy.

This book is not here to judge you, diagnose you, or tell you to "just be positive." It's not here to minimize your pain or rush your healing. It's here to sit with you in the truth of what depression actually feels like, and to help you take your power back from it, one day at a time.

I wrote this because I reached a point where I realized something important: depression may be loud, persistent, and convincing, but it is not the boss of me. And it doesn't get to be the boss of you either.

Snatching your life back doesn't happen all at once. It happens in small decisions. In awareness. In learning how to interrupt the lies your mind tells you when you're tired and hurting. It happens when you stop identifying yourself as broken and start recognizing that you've been wounded, and wounds can heal.

Inside these pages, I'm sharing what I've lived, what I've learned, and what helped me climb out of some very dark places. I'm not speaking from theory. I'm speaking from experience. From the moments when getting through the day felt like the biggest victory. From the times when faith felt quiet, hope felt distant, and I had to relearn how to talk to myself with honesty and compassion.

This book is not about perfection. It's about choosing to keep going, even when your heart feels heavy.

You don't have to agree with everything I say, but know that I know the pain of depression personally. I have been there and it can gets better, so please do not give up.

Most of all, know this: you are not alone, you are not weak, and you are not beyond help. The fact that you're here means there is still a part of you that wants to live a happy fulfilling life again.

Let's start snatching your life back, together.

1

First Step is…

Depression doesn't just sit on your chest, it talks. It narrates. It comments on everything you do and everything you don't do. It turns your mind into a courtroom where you're always the one on trial, always the one being questioned, always the one being found guilty. And if you don't recognize that voice for what it is, you'll start treating its opinions like facts. You'll start believing that your worst thoughts are the truest version of you. But they're not. They are symptoms. They are echoes. They are learned patterns. And patterns can be interrupted.

Whether you can accept it or not, you taught yourself how to belittle and disrespect you. You are leading the charge on the only attacks against you that truly matter, because the attacks from the outside world are far less damaging than the ones you do to yourself. There is an old African proverb that says, "If there is no enemy on the inside, the enemy on the outside can do you no harm." When I speak motivationally, I always introduce this quote to the audience. It is short, but it is so very powerful if you allow it to sink in. There is no damage greater than the self-inflicted pain we cause ourselves. The internal enemy does more damage than any outside enemy ever could. We can be our own worst enemy, the masters of self- sabotage. For example, no one ever walked up to me and reminded me that I was an abandoned child. I did that. I told myself repeatedly that I was not worthy because my own mother did not want me. I now know that was a lie. Her drug addiction and the choices she made during it had nothing to do with me. But choosing to take it personally caused me over forty years of pain. This book was written to help you avoid that.

That is exactly how a thought cycle works. A thought cycle is not just "thinking negative." It's repetition coupled with belief. It's the same sentence in different outfits. It's the same fear wearing different faces. It's your mind automatically reaching for the worst-case scenario because somewhere along the way, pain trained you to expect pain. It's waking up and already feeling defeated. It's remembering one mistake and using it as evidence that *you* are a mistake. It's replaying a conversation from five years ago like it happened this morning. It's looking in the mirror and hearing criticism instead of compassion. Depression loves cycles because cycles keep you stuck. When you're stuck, you don't move. When you don't move, you don't change. And when you don't change, depression feels safe and hangs around for much longer. this applies to the strongest of men and even innocent children, Depression does not just strike woman. Anyone can experience it.

The reason this matters so much is because depression doesn't always start with what people do to you; sometimes it deepens because of what you keep saying to you. It's the private narrative you repeat when nobody else is around. It's the labels you place on yourself. It's the meaning you attach to what happened to you. It's the way you interpret rejection, disappointment, delay, and pain. When you repeatedly agree with the worst interpretation, your mind starts building a home there. It becomes familiar. It becomes your default. And then you don't even realize you're living under attack, because you have called the attack "truth."

Unfortunately, I witnessed a murder at a very young age. My beloved grandmother was killed right in front of me by her husband of thirty-two years. I lived with them after my own mother tried to kill me as a three-month-old baby by putting me into a suitcase and closing it. My grandmother was amazing, she raised me and my older sister as her own, and she loved us dearly. When I was seventeen, my grandfather shot her in the head in front of me. That was the day my life changed, and I'm sure it was the source, along with the maternal abandonment, of my early onset of depression. I suffered for many years with PTSD, which is **Post-Traumatic Stress Disorder**, and depression. I did not begin the journey of healing until my late thirties because I did not know I could heal from something that horrendous. But I did, and you can too.

Because the moment you recognize the enemy on the inside, you also recognize your power. If your words helped create the prison, your words can also help build the exit. If your mind learned to repeat the lie, your mind can also be trained to repeat the truth. That's why the work is not just about "feeling better," it's about thinking better on purpose. It's about catching the sentence before it becomes a cycle. It's about interrupting the old story before it talks you out of your future, it's about finally giving yourself what you should have been giving yourself all along: compassion, understanding, grace, and a new narrative that leads you toward healing instead of keeping you stuck in the pain of the past.

But your mind was not created to be a prison. Your mind was created to be a garden. And if you've ever tried to grow anything, you know this: whatever you water will grow. Whatever you ignore will either die or become overrun with weeds. Depression is a weed that multiplies when it's left unchecked. It spreads through the quiet moments. It spreads through shame. It spreads through exhaustion. It spreads through isolation. And then one day you look up and it feels like your whole inner world is covered in it. That doesn't mean the garden is ruined. It means it needs tending. It means you need tools. It means you need a new rhythm.

Breaking the thought cycle begins with one brave moment of honesty. You have to catch the thought in the act. I call it *"Catch and Cast." I'm pretty sure i have a few videos on YouTube with that title.* Catch that negative thought and cast it right on out of your head. then replace it with a new empowering, uplifting thought. A Thought that makes you feel great about yourself. Catch it quickly not after it's already dragged you into a mood. Not after it's already ruined your whole day. Not after you've already spiraled into the "what's the point" place. You have to learn to notice the moment the narrative starts. Depression usually begins with a simple sentence. "I'm tired." "I can't do this." "Nobody cares." "Nothing ever changes." "What's wrong with me?" These sentences sound normal because they're familiar. Familiar doesn't mean true. Familiar just means rehearsed. It is something that you have done repeatedly. It means something is already embedded into your subconscious.

The enemy of healing is automatic thinking. Automatic thinking is when your mind responds before you even ask it to. Something goes wrong, and immediately your mind says, "Of course." Someone doesn't call back, and immediately your mind says, "See, nobody wants me" You wake up heavy, and immediately your mind says, "Today is going to be terrible." That's the cycle. It's not just the thought. It's the speed of the thought. The thought arrives like it owns the place, and you accept it like it pays rent. But the truth is, you don't have to agree with every thought that visits you.

There is power in pausing, taking a deep breath. It's a spiritual kind of power. A holy kind of power. A positive tool we all should use. Because a pause gives you space to breathe, and a breathing gives you space to think and choose your response. Depression wants you to react. It wants you to accept. It wants you to surrender. But when you pause, you disrupt the pattern. You begin to take your authority back. You begin to say, "Wait a minute. That is a thought. That is not a prophecy. That is a feeling. That is not my future. That is a memory. That is not my identity." You can then make a conscious choice to cast the negativity right on out of there.

Some people think faith means you never have negative thoughts. That's not faith. That's denial. Faith is what you do when the negative thoughts show up. This is when you practice the tools you will learn in this book. Faith is what you choose to agree with. Faith is deciding that God's voice is louder than depression's voice, even if you can't feel it yet. Faith is saying, "I might feel low, but I am not forsaken." Faith is saying, "My mind is loud, but God is still present." Faith is saying, "I am not my thoughts, and I will not let my thoughts lead me."

Depression tries to make you speak against yourself. It tries to make you curse your future with your mouth. It tries to make you describe your life in a way that keeps you trapped. It wants you to say, "I'll never be happy." "I'll never be normal."

"I'll never heal." And when you repeat those sentences, your spirit begins to memorize them. Your body begins to respond to them. Your choices begin to follow them. Words are not just sounds. Words are seeds. And one of the most life-changing decisions you can make is to stop planting seeds that grow more darkness. You are the gardener of your life. You must decide what you will plant.

Breaking the thought cycle is not pretending everything is fine. It's telling the truth with power. It's saying, "This is hard, but it is not hopeless." It's saying, "I feel heavy, but I am still moving." It's saying, "I'm struggling today, but I will not quit on myself." It's saying, "I'm not where I want to be, but I am not where I used to be." It's giving your mind a new sentence to repeat. Not a fake sentence. A strengthening sentence. A sentence with backbone. A sentence with spirit. A sentence that represents your understanding that there is a universal law of Eb and Flow. Bad times will not last forever. God designed everything to have a season. Depression is a season that will pass.

I teach my children to record positive affirmations on their cell phones and drift off to sleep while listening to them. That is a tool I used to implant the positive thoughts into my subconscious mind. It works.

You have to understand this about your brain: repetition creates grooves. The more you think a thought, the easier it becomes to think that thought again. You can choose to stop thinking a specific thought. Find uplifting things that distract you. Create positive habitual habits and eventually they will become second nature.

Depression feels like it has momentum. It does because you have been doing it consistently for years sometimes. It has been practiced. It has been accepted as belief. But the same rule works for healing. The more you practice a new thought, the more natural it becomes. The more you speak life, the more your mind starts to recognize life. The more you choose self-compassion, the more your nervous system begins to calm. This is not just motivational talk. This is how your mind is wired. Depression did not become strong overnight, and healing does not become strong overnight. But it does become strong.

There will be days when the thought cycle feels like a wave you can't stop. On those days, your goal is not to win with perfection. Your goal is to win with interruption. Even if you only interrupt the cycle for a minute, that minute matters. Even if all you can say is, "Not today Satan" Even if all you can do is breathe and whisper, "God help me." Even if all you can manage is to get out of bed and sit up. Interruption is a victory. It is proof that you are still in the fight. As long as you have breath in your body the fight is not over. Each day you awake you are presented with a new opportunity to *"Kick Depression in the Butt"*

Depression loves isolation because isolation gives it a microphone. When you're alone too long, your thoughts get louder. Your fear gets creative. Your shame gets persuasive. So part of breaking the cycle is refusing to disappear. It's choosing connection even when you don't feel like talking. It's letting one safe person know you're not okay. It's refusing to pretend. It's allowing support to touch you. It letting that supportive family member hug you. Because healing is not just personal, it is relational. Even when depression says, "Stay away," you have to remember that love is medicine.

And listen, there is nothing wrong with getting professional help. There is nothing un-spiritual about therapy. I had many therapist when I was suffering with depression. There is nothing weak about medication if you need it. God works through people. God works through wisdom. God works through tools. Sometimes healing is prayer and breath. Sometimes healing is prayer and boundaries. Sometimes healing is prayer and a counselor. Sometimes healing is prayer and learning how to sleep again or laugh again. You do not have to choose between faith and help. You can hold both. You can be spiritual and still need support. You can love God and still need a practical plan.

Breaking the thought cycle also means forgiving yourself for having the cycle in the first place. Some of you feel guilty for being depressed, and that guilt becomes another layer of pain. You feel bad for feeling bad. You criticize yourself for struggling. You compare your private battle to someone else's public smile. That is not healing. That is self-harm in a polite outfit. You deserve tenderness. You deserve patience. You deserve compassion. And the same grace you give everyone else is the grace you must learn to give yourself.

I named my first book **My Spiritual Smile** for a reason. At the time, I was running a successful business in Los Angeles called **Braids By SaBrina**, and I had several young women from similar backgrounds working for me. I was also raising children alone, so I learned how to keep going no matter what. I became the kind of woman who could handle business, take care of everybody, and still show up with a smile. I was always smiling on the outside. But on the inside, I was broken. My inner joy, my spiritual smile I would not find until much later in life.

I had suppressed witnessing the murder of my grandmother. I never spoke about it in the first ten years after it happened, and I carried that silence like it was normal. I got married young and lived my life as if nothing had ever happened to me, as if I could just keep moving forward and outpace the pain. I tried to live like the past didn't exist, like trauma could be buried and never resurface. But trauma doesn't disappear just because you don't talk about it. It waits. It hides. And as time went on, everything I had suppressed began to surface as anger.

I can't go back and do things differently, but I can choose what I do with my story now. And if this book can help others deal with their trauma and hurt differently, then I have done my job. No matter who you are or what you have been through, you can heal, and you do not have to carry that pain with you for life. You deserve to live a happy, fulfilling life.

Here's what I want you to keep with you as you move forward. You are not powerless in your own mind. Thoughts will come up without warning, and that's part of being human. What you do have control over is which thoughts you give your time and energy to. You are allowed to decide that your mind will no longer be a place where you feel attacked or overwhelmed all day.

This is something you learn slowly, not perfectly. It is a process but a beautiful one. When you notice a thought that hurts you and you choose not to sit with it. When you choose to cast it out and replace it with a thought that makes you feel good, you are winning the war on depression. It happens when you stop repeating old beliefs about yourself and start speaking with a little more kindness and patience. Treating yourself with love and care is not giving up. It's giving yourself a chance. You will get better at it. The pain will subside and you will eventually master uplifting yourself.

Over time, you may look back and realize things feel different. You feel better. Not because every suddenly day became easy, but because you stopped letting the hard moments take over your life. Change comes from small choices made again and again. Each pause, each redirected thought, each moment you stay present instead of spiraling helped create that mental and emotional shift.

This is how healing begins to take root. It grows through consistency and your compassion for yourself. You are still here, and the opportunity for a great life still exist. Keep choosing yourself, even on the hard days. Your life belongs to you, and depression does not get to decide how this story ends.

2

What Depression Really Feels Like

People talk about depression like it's one thing. Like it has one look, one sound, one definition. But if you've ever lived inside it, you know better. Depression doesn't show up the same way for everyone, and it doesn't always announce itself when it arrives.

Sometimes it doesn't feel like sadness at all. Sometimes it feels like emptiness. Or heaviness. Or exhaustion that sleep doesn't fix. It can feel like your body is present, but your joy didn't make it out of bed with you. Like you're moving through the day on autopilot, smiling when required, answering questions on cue, while something inside you keeps whispering, *I'm tired of pretending.*

When depression settles in, hope feels distant. Love feels conditional. Faith feels quiet. You may even start believing God isn't listening anymore—or worse, that you've somehow been forgotten. Those thoughts can feel terrifying, isolating, and deeply personal. I want to say this first, before we go any further: **those feelings are real, and they are valid.** They don't make you weak. They don't make you broken. And they are not permanent.

There is another side to this. Even if you can't see it yet.

Depression doesn't always scream. Sometimes it whispers. It disguises itself as "I'm just overwhelmed" or "I'm just tired." It hides behind responsibility and survival mode. You keep showing up. You keep handling business. You keep caring for everyone else. Meanwhile, inside, you feel like you're slowly disappearing.

That's how it was for me.

In my early twenties, depression was already a familiar companion, even though I didn't have a name for it yet. I was a young Black woman from Compton, California, raised in circumstances that taught me how to survive long before they taught me how to feel safe. Both of my parents struggled with substance abuse. My father, Jesse Paul Fisher, loved me deeply— but alcohol had a stronger grip on him. He passed away from alcohol-related illness when I was ten years old.

My mother was physically present in the world, but emotionally absent in my life. My sister Mary and I were the oldest of six children, and although we were blessed to be raised by our grandmother, Ella Mae Fisher Fair—a woman who loved us fiercely—the wound of being unwanted by my biological mother never healed quietly. It planted itself deep inside me.

I didn't walk around calling it depression. I didn't know that word applied to me. I just knew I felt unwanted. Unworthy. Like something about me was fundamentally wrong. I learned how to smile anyway. I learned how to function anyway. But inside, I felt hollow.

That's one of the cruelest things about depression—it can exist quietly while life keeps moving. You can laugh. You can dress well. You can be productive. You can take care of everyone else. And still feel completely empty inside. Like you're existing instead of living. Like something precious was taken from you, and you don't know when it happened or how to get it back.

Depression also has a way of piling guilt on top of pain. You start judging yourself for struggling. Everyday tasks feel overwhelming. Returning a text feels impossible. Showering becomes optional. Eating feels complicated. Brain fog makes decisions exhausting. And then the inner critic shows up and asks, *Why can't you just do it?*

That voice is not telling the truth.

I remember living in Los Angeles on 109th and Normandie. I was young, newly separated from my first husband, and already carrying more emotional weight than I had language for. I married at nineteen, far too young to understand boundaries, self-worth, or what love should actually look like. I was still trying to heal abandonment wounds I didn't know how to name, and instead, I walked straight into a relationship that added new trauma on top of old pain.

Depression thrives in environments where pain goes unspoken.

Here's something that changed everything for me: **depression is not who you are.** It's not your personality. It's not your identity. It's not your truth. It is an intruder. It is a liar and a thief that feeds on the stories you tell yourself when you are in pain.

For years, I believed the lie that if my own mother didn't want me, that I was worthless. That lie shaped my choices. My relationships. My expectations. And when you're young and still forming your sense of self, those lies can sound like facts.

Depression is sneaky like that. It doesn't knock on the door and introduce itself. It blends into your exhaustion. It hides behind your stress. It convinces you that solutions don't exist.

That the future is closed. That the light is gone for good.

But depression is common, far more common than most people realize. Millions of people are walking around every day carrying invisible battles. When depression goes unrecognized or untreated for too long, it can become dangerous. Not because people want to die, but because they get tired of living in pain that feels endless.

That's why I'm writing this book. Because there is another ending available.

If you ever find yourself in a place where life feels unbearable, please reach out for help. In the United States, you can call or text **988**, the Suicide & Crisis Lifeline. If you're outside the U.S., your local emergency services can help you immediately. Asking for help is not weakness, It is self-preservation.

Spiritually, depression can feel like separation, from God, from hope, from yourself. It can convince you that your prayers are pointless, that you're being punished, or that you're too far gone for help. I understand what that feels like. But I want you to hear this clearly: It does get better. **Your feelings are valid, but they are not always feeding you the truth.**

There is a little voice inside all of us that narrates our lives. When we are depressed that voice takes hold of our mind and our thoughts become distorted. The voice is very convincing. You believe that is is *you*. But that's hurt and pain talking, not truth.

The beautiful thing is this: that voice can be retrained. The same expansive mind that learned fear can learn love, peace and safety. The mind that learned self sabotage can learn possibility and hope. The inner dialogue that once tore you down can be taught to encourage you and build you back up.

There will be seasons when your emotions are louder than

your faith. That doesn't mean you are failing. It means you are a human being, so be patient with yourself. Depression doesn't make a weak person, you've been wounded like many of us, and wounds need love and care, not ridicule.

Depression often grows from unprocessed grief, childhood trauma, betrayal, rejection, abuse, chronic stress, or the pressure of being everything for everyone else. Sometimes it's chemical. Sometimes it's situational. Often, it's layered. That's why pretending it doesn't exist never works.

At some point, you have to stop running from it and turn around and face it. Because what you don't confront will keep controlling you.

Here's the shift this book is inviting you into: ***Depression is Not the Boss of You.*** It does not get to control your life. Depression does not get the final say. You can chose to retrain your mind and replace all those negative thoughts with positive uplifting ones.

This chapter is your line in the sand. You're not lazy, you are depleted mentally, spiritually and emotionally. You are still w wonderful being, underneath all the heaviness and fog, I believe, with everything in me, that the real you is still there, waiting to breathe again.

This is where we start snatching your life back. Not all at once, but one day at a time.

3

The Pain Behind The Smile

There is a special kind of pain that comes from being the one everyone thinks is okay, and that has always been me. I was the owner of **Braids By SaBrina** for over twenty-six years, and I always had younger women working for me who looked to me for leadership. Most of them had no idea about the tragedies I had been through. I wasn't intentionally hiding anything; I had simply buried that pain so far down that sometimes I forgot it was even there. I was the consistent one who showed up daily, opened the door for my staff, and provided them a place to make a living. I was the leader, the one who kept it together. The one who still took care of business, still cracked jokes, still posted pictures, and still said, "I'm good."

Meanwhile, I was quietly falling apart on the inside. I was smiling with tears behind my eyes. I was laughing while my chest felt tight. I was being strong because I did not feel like I had permission to be anything else. And after a while, that kind of strength starts to feel like a prison. When pain is buried long enough, it doesn't disappear, it builds pressure. And eventually, it will erupt like a volcano and spill out into your life.

Some people do not realize how exhausting it is to pretend. They think the smile means you are fine. They think the productivity means you are healed. They think the fact that you are functioning means you are not hurting. But depression does not always take you out of the world; sometimes it keeps you in the world, performing. You are physically present, but emotionally somewhere far away. You are doing what you have to do, but you are not fully experiencing the life you are living. And that is why so many people suffer in silence, because the outside looks normal, but the inside is heavy. In this book, I'm going to show you how I finally changed that. Healing is possible for everyone. Yes, prayer is important but you must get up and do the work. Fight for your happiness and peace.

Smiling while you are suffering often starts as survival. You learned early how to keep going. You learned how to push through and be dependable. You swallow pain and still show up looking polished for everyone else.. You train yourself to keep your tears private, to clean your face, and walk back into the room like nothing happened. At first, that skill helps you out a lot, it protects you. It gets you through. But then it becomes a habit. A lifestyle. A personality trait. Then one day, you do not even know how to tell the truth about how you are really feeling anymore because you have practiced being okay more than you have practiced being honest.

I remember the few times, as a young woman, that I actually let it all out. I cried, and I told someone about the abandonment and abuse from my mother, and about the murder of my grandmother. At first, they seemed loving and compassionate, like they were truly listening. But by the time I got to the end of the story, the look on their face registered to me as, "Wow… that's a big one. I don't know if I can help you with that." It crushed me.

No one knew how to tell a young woman who watched her grandmother's head blown off by her grandfather that everything was going to be okay, and it showed in their eyes. It felt like they quietly wrote me off as permanently broken. Because I could see and feel that distance in them, I retreated even farther inside, vowing never to speak of those things again. It hurt me, and it taught me that sharing my past was not a safe space.

After that, I started editing myself before I even opened my mouth. I learned how to tell the "acceptable" version of my story, the one that didn't make people uncomfortable, the one that didn't change the energy in the room. I learned how to keep the hardest parts locked away behind a smile, because it felt safer to carry the pain alone than to watch someone's face shift again. I didn't want pity. I didn't want someone to fix me. I just wanted to be heard without feeling like my truth was too heavy to hold. But when you don't have language for trauma, and the people around you don't have understanding for it either, silence starts to feel like the only option.

The more I stayed silent, the more isolated I became on the inside. I could be surrounded by people and still feel completely alone, because no one was meeting the real me, only the version of me I served them. I had given up on healing. I lived with the nightmare of the murder and figured I would forever. I became skilled at surviving, but I didn't know how to be safe. I became skilled at functioning, but I didn't know how to be free. That kind of loneliness is its own kind of pain, because it convinces you that if people really knew what you carried, they would step back. It makes you believe that your story disqualifies you from love, from peace, from joy. And that is how trauma deepens, when you start carrying it not only as a memory, but as a secret.

Because of the tragedy, and because I was out in the world at a young age trying to navigate life with more pain than guidance, I got married at nineteen to my 12th-grade boyfriend. He was older than me and a great provider, and the truth is, I didn't have anywhere else to go. My older sister was away at college in San Diego. Our father had died when we were ten and eleven. Our mother was still out in the world, addicted to drugs. And we had lost the one stable home we had ever known, the home filled with love and security with our grandparents, when our grandfather killed our grandmother.

At the time, I believed I loved my first husband. But what does a nineteen-year-old with PTSD and abandonment issues truly know about love? When you've lived through trauma, love can start to feel like safety, and safety can start to feel like rescue. Sometimes you don't choose marriage because you're ready; sometimes you choose it because you're trying to survive. Sometimes you aren't looking for a partner as much as you're looking for a place to land. And I was looking for somewhere, anywhere, that didn't feel like loss.

So in August of 1989, I married **Clyde Arnold Reece**. my first child an dour only son Justin Clyde Reece was born a few months earlier on February 18, 1989. I carried into that marriage not just a dream for a better life, but also a whole history of grief, fear, and survival that I didn't yet have the words to explain. I was trying to build a future while still bleeding from the past, and I didn't know then what I know now: unhealed pain doesn't disappear just because you put on a wedding dress.

There is a deeper layer that many people do not talk about. Smiling while suffering can become a way of avoiding what you really feel. Because if you slow down, you might have to face the grief you buried. If you stop moving, you might have to admit you are lonely. If you tell the truth, you might have to accept that you are tired of holding everything together. Sometimes the smile is not just for others. Sometimes it is for you. Sometimes it is the cover you put over your own pain so you do not have to look at it.

But your soul knows. Your body and your spirit know. Eventually, the weight shows up somewhere. It shows up in anxiety. It shows up in extreme erratic behavior, It shows up in irritable sleepless nights. It shows up in exhaustion that rest does not fix. For some it shows up in losing motivation, in feeling numb. The moments when you are alone and the mask finally slips, and you realize you have been holding your breath emotionally for a long time.

Spiritually, this chapter matters because depression loves hidden places. It thrives in secrecy. It grows in silence. It gets stronger when you feel like you have to protect everyone else from the truth of what you are going through. But healing happens in the light. It happens when you stop trying to look strong and start allowing yourself to get supported by the ones who love you. Healing happens when you admit, even to God, that you are not okay. Not as a dramatic statement, but as an honest one. Because God cannot heal what you keep denying. God cannot comfort the version of you that is always pretending. God meets you in truth. Truth and acknowledgment is the first step towards a better life. I tell my kids all the time.

I will never be depressed again. That can become truth for you as well. Not because life will stop presenting challenges. But because you will now have the tools as I did, the tools to drag yourself up and out of that bed and take charge of your own future. You will have the daily practical tools to uplift and encourage yourself.

Some of you have been using faith as another mask. You have been saying the right spiritual words while your heart is breaking. You go around quoting scriptures while your mind is spiraling. You tell everyone to trust God while, privately, you feel abandoned by God. You feel like you are not allowed to struggle because you love God. But faith is not the absence of pain. Faith is what you cling to while you are in pain. There is nothing wrong with saying, "God, I love You, but I am hurting." "God, I believe, but I am tired." "God, I know You are real, but I do not feel You right now." That is not weak. That is real and honest. And real is where healing begins.

God has already instilled the help you need inside of you. Faith without works is dead. You must get up and stop looking to the sky, waiting for the heavens to open and for God to descend and give you the answers. You have them already, inside of you. The Kingdom of Heaven is inside of you already. You have to initiate the healing and stop depending on the pastor or the therapist to do it for you.

Get up right now, whether you are a man, woman, or child. Walk over to the mirror and look at yourself. Take a deep, long breath. Say, "I am ready, now." "No more suffering for me." "I am healed and happy, from this day forward." Speak it with emotion, passion, and certainty, and as sure as my name is **SaBrina Fisher Romania Reece**, it will become your reality. Speak it now. Live it later. Do not give up.

Make this a daily ritual, speaking as if the healing has already taken place. Let it apply to your mental, physical, emotional, financial, and spiritual healing.

It's ok to smile outwardly while doing the work needed

inwardly. Smiling while suffering is also connected to the role you play in other people's lives. Maybe you are the strong one in your family. Maybe you are the helper. The provider. The one people call when they need advice. The one who is always there. When you are that person, it can feel like you are not allowed to fall apart. You might think, If I break, everything breaks. So you keep going. You keep carrying. You keep showing up. But you were never meant to carry everybody and carry yourself through depression at the same time. That is too much for any human being. Keep Smiling because that invites a positive healing energy into your life but make sure you are actively doing the work needed to smile from the inside as well.

There is a difference between being strong and being silent. You do not owe the whole world your story, but you do owe yourself honesty. You deserve to have at least one safe space where you can productively release and let go. There should be at least one person who can hear your truth without judging you. You deserve to have a moments where you are not performing. Simply time to spend with your mind to check in a make sure you are OK.

Stop viewing crying a negative. Crying a a natural and healthy release. Try to change your perception and view every tear as a release of pain, toxins and stress from your life.

One of the biggest lies depression tells us that we are a burden. At times it tells you that if you speak up, you will bother people. It can make you feel that if you admit you are struggling, you will disappoint others. Depression tells you that your pain makes you too much to deal with. But the truth is, the people who truly love you would rather know how they can help you, than to see you in pain of even lose you. The people who truly love you would rather hear the truth than keep watching you drag yourself through life. Even if some people do not understand, that does not mean your truth is wrong. There are so many people suffering through depression. Reach out and give them the hug that you need in those moments.

This chapter is your permission slip to stop pretending you are OK, when you need help. Not because you hopeless and have given up, but because you are ready to feel better about life. Healing from depression is possible for everyone seeking it.

I also want to be responsible and clear about something important. If you have been prescribed medication from a doctor, please take the medication you were prescribed. If you are under the care of a physician or therapist, please follow their guidance and their treatment plan. Keep all of your appointments. Be honest about how you are feeling. Get professional help when you need it, and do not stop medication suddenly or change your dosage without talking to your doctor. There is no shame in using medical support as a part of your healing. Couple that with the positive tools you are learning in this book. You have the ultimate control over your mental and emotional health. It starts with simply getting out of bed each day and deciding it will be a great day.

I want you to understand that medication and therapy are not meant to replace you, they are meant to support you. They can help stabilize you, guide you, and give you tools, but the key to full healing still involves your participation. Combined with medical care, you must do the internal work yourself. You must take ownership of your thoughts, your habits, your boundaries, and the way you speak to yourself when no one else is around. You have to choose healing daily, not just when you feel strong, but especially when you feel tired.

That is why I am so serious about the mind. Mind is all and most of our suffering begins there. I'm encouraging you to speak your affirmations everyday. I realize they may feel like lies at first, especially if you've been living in pain for a long time. But trust me, eventually they will not. You are not speaking affirmations to ignore reality; you are speaking them to interrupt the lies depression repeats and to train your mind to come into agreement with hope and possibility. Over time, your mindset will shift. You will begin to feel better and think differently.

Yes, make sure you do the professional work, but please do the personal internal work. Let your doctor help you. Let your therapist guide you if they can. Let medication, when needed, support your brain and body. But also show up for your own healing with consistency and intention. You take full responsibility of your own mind, body and soul. Because nobody can live your life for you. Nobody can make your daily choices for you, and when you combine medical support with personal responsibility, you stop waiting to be rescued and you start rebuilding, one truth, one tool, one day at a time.

There is something very powerful that happens when you stop faking like you are happy and truly do the work needed to create authentic joy in your life.

You do not have to wear the mask forever. You can be honest about your feelings. You can be a work in progress that understands that this is a daily battle, but a battle that you can win.

The strongest people are not the ones who never get down or sad. The strongest people are the ones who stop pretending and start seeking freedom. These people are the ones who decide they deserve a life that feels good on the inside, not just a life that looks good on the outside.

4

The Root

Depression rarely shows up as a random visitor. Sometimes it does, but more often it arrives carrying history. It arrives with receipts. It arrives with memories your mind tried to pack away so you could keep functioning. It arrives with old pain that never got a safe place to land. And this is why healing is not just about "feeling better." Healing is about telling the truth and finding the root cause. Not the polite truth. Not the version that keeps everybody comfortable. The truth that explains why your body reacts the way it reacts, why your heart shuts down, why your mind spirals, why certain situations make you feel like you are back in a place you promised yourself you would never return to.

Unfortunately, in many families there are secrets. It does not matter the nationality or economic status. Those old, buried secrets are still causing someone, right now, to not live up to their full potential in life. I'm in no way suggesting having hurtful, explosive conversations with family that most likely won't prove to be fruitful anyway. I'm suggesting having those conversations with yourself. Digging deep within. Who are

26

you mad at? Who hurt you? Who violated you? Who devalued you? You must identify the root so you can kill it.

For years, I waited on my mother to find me and tell me that she loved me, and that she was so sorry. I waited eagerly, believing that she held the key to my happiness, but she never came. When I finally gathered the courage to go to her, hoping she would fix me, I realized she was incapable of doing so.

I will never forget the day I walked up the cement walkway to her apartment. I was 45 years old. The sun was beaming down on my face, and my heart was pounding so hard in my chest. I reached the front door and lightly knocked, but no one answered. I knocked a second time, and a faint voice said, "Who is it?" I nervously replied, "It's me. It's SaBrina, your daughter."

One of my younger sisters opened the door and let me inside. My mother, who had in recent years gone blind, sat on a couch in the living room. My sister pulled up a chair for me near my mother, and then she sat across from the both of us. My younger sister then turned to me and warned me to stay calm. The me that she remembered was filled with anger and rage for our mother.

I anticipated that this would be a long, emotional conversation, and I didn't want to forget the details, so I brought a small tape recorder.

I turned the recorder on and began to ask my mother a series of questions: "How did you meet my father?" "Who introduced you to drugs?" "Were you abused as a child?" "How could you abandon and abuse six children?" "Did your parents love you?"

Finally, I asked the most important question of all: "Did you really put me into a suitcase as a three-month-old baby with the intent to take my life?"

I sat there in silence, eagerly awaiting an answer. I knew that this would be the day I had been dreaming of for years. I just knew that she would cry and embrace me and tell me no, she would never do that, and that I had been lied to all these years. I waited for her to say that she was sorry for not being there, and for allowing drugs to cause her to leave and hurt all six of her children.

Instead, she looked in my direction and said, "Yes. Yes, I did put you into a suitcase because you cried too damn much as a baby."

My heart sank. Time seemed to stand still. I could not believe what I was hearing. Although I had already been told the story and hated her for it, I just knew that she would tell me it wasn't true and give me what I would serve as an acceptable response to my question, a response that would make me finally feel whole, a response that would make it easy for me to understand her actions. That was not the case. My heart broke, and in that moment, the pain seemed unbearable.

I took a deep breath and looked directly at her, and I said something I never imagined I would say to her: "I forgive you."

Something that I can't fully explain, some divine force, in that moment, gave me the comfort and the knowledge that I was sent there for myself and not for her. No sooner than the pain of her response hit, something else, which I call the "Divine source of love, God" made me instantly realize that I was sent there to release the pain and resentment I'd held for her, because it was preventing me from fully loving myself. I realized that her actions had nothing to do with me. I had no control over if or when she would ever deal with and rectify her behavior. I knew then that from that day forward, I could not depend on her to make me feel loved and worthy of life. It was up to me, and holding on to the anger and pain was preventing me from returning to my true, God-given nature of love. Human beings can not heal you.

When I walked out of that apartment, it felt like I was seeing the beauty of the world for the very first time. Not because she gave me hugs and tears of love and regret or gave me all the answers I needed. But because I now understood why I was so compelled to go, and that God needed me to understand and take charge of my role in my own healing.

As I was leaving I glanced at the grass, which seemed to be a brighter green. I looked up at the sky, and it seemed to be a beautiful, radiant blue that I had never noticed before. It's apparent to me now that making the choice to forgive my mother, despite her never having said the long-awaited words that I expected her to say, was the only true way for me to grow. Even though she never begged for my forgiveness, embraced me, or showered me with the love I thought I could not survive without, forgiveness changed my life. Making the choice to forgive her, even though she never asked, was not easy, but in that moment I knew it was what I had to do for me. I decided that day that even if I never saw her again, I had forgiven her and was finally ready to move forward and learn to truly love myself, which was one of the best decisions I have ever made. It is what I want for each and every one of you. That weight can finally be lifted and you can experience a wonderful life.

The thought of my mother was always a trigger for me. Her very name, Shirley Ann Tillman always brought me to tears instantly and even made me anger. A trigger is not weakness, it is evidence. It is your nervous system remembering what your mouth may not say out loud. It is your brain recognizing danger based on past experiences, even when the danger is no longer in the room. Triggers can be obvious, like a specific place, a smell, a tone of voice, a holiday, a song, a certain time of year. But triggers can also be quiet and confusing. It can be someone not texting back or a change in someone's energy. It can be conflict or feeling ignored. It can even be love, because love can feel unsafe when you have known abandonment. It can also be success, because success sometimes reminds you of who never clapped for you.

I have definitely dealt with being super successful and still feeling hurt when others did not clap for me. It's normal to expect the ones who say they love you to celebrate you, to speak the words of congratulations, to show up with support, but they do not always say them. They do not always show up for you. That is why you must learn to congratulate yourself. I have written twelve or more self-help books, spoken motivationally as the keynote speaker at over 40 events, sustained a business where I employed over 1700 women for 30 years and when I post any of my accomplishments online hoping for support, I get crickets, especially from the people closest to me. I laugh at it now, but it can still be hurtful. What's interesting is that if I post something that makes people think I'm in distress, just from the dramatic title I chose , Wah-La!, all of a sudden there are hundreds of responses. I don't have time to figure out why the world sometimes prefers trauma over triumph, or negative over positive, but I do know this: it can be disappointing, and it can trigger those old self-worth feelings to rise up again. Don't let it. Don't let the silence of others talk you out of your confidence. Don't let a lack of applause make you question your value.

Because when you are triggered, the emotion you feel in the moment is often bigger than the moment itself. That's how you know something deeper is underneath it. You are not "overreacting", you are reacting to layers. You are reacting to old grief, old fear, old rejection, old humiliation, old pain. You are reacting to the parts of you that learned to protect themselves by staying on guard. Your mind and body have been trying to keep you safe the best way they know how. Sometimes that protection looks like anger. Sometimes it looks like shutting down. Sometimes it looks like needing control. Sometimes it looks like people pleasing. Sometimes it looks like perfectionism. Sometimes it looks like numbness. Sometimes it looks like depression.

Trauma is not just what happened. Trauma is what happened inside you because of what happened to you. It is the wound you carry after the event is over. It is the way your body learned to brace itself. It is the way your heart learned to expect disappointment. It is the way your mind learned to prepare for the next blow. Trauma can come from big events, like abuse, violence, loss, betrayal, accidents, neglect. But trauma can also come from repeated emotional experiences that taught you the same painful message over and over. Being dismissed and unheard. Being criticized or shamed. Being compared. Being chosen last. Being loved inconsistently. Being forced to grow up too fast. Being treated like your feelings were an inconvenience.

Sometimes the root is not one moment. Sometimes the root is a long season in your life. Possibly a season where you were surviving, and you did not have time to feel true emotions. A season where you kept going because you had to, and now your body is collecting the debt. Depression can be that debt. It can be what shows up when the adrenaline wears off, or what happens after you have been strong for too long. It can be your soul finally saying, I cannot keep doing this without care. Stop and fuel your own mind, body and spirit before you move forward in life. fill up your own cup because you matter most.

Finding the root is not about blaming others the past. It is about understanding yourself. Learning to have compassion for yourself. It is about gaining the wisdom needed to heal and prosper. if you do not know where the pain started, you will keep trying to treat symptoms while the wound stays open. You will keep trying to "think positive" while your nervous system is still living in survival mode. You will pray away what requires healing, support, and tools. Faith is powerful, but faith does not mean ignoring the root. Faith can also mean facing it with God beside you. I call those roots "Holes" we must identify what caused them, face it head on, forgive it and then leave it in the past.

I did not start seriously digging for the root cause of my pain until I was in my late thirties. I knew the two main incidents that traumatized me but I did not know how they were directly affecting my current life. I think my past left me with what I call "Holes" in my heart and soul and I did not know how to close them.

Unfortunately this world is filled with hurt people; people who have endured pain, death, loss, tragedy and disappointments of all kinds. I used to believe that I was alone in my despair and that my particular situation was rare. I thought no one else had experienced and could never understand it, so I never spoke about it. I was ashamed and I thought people would view me in a different light because of my past. Because I was unwanted and had been rejected by my mother, naturally I thought I would be rejected by the world in general. I always had my defenses up, which translated as attitude and reinforced the "angry black girl" trope for many. I was ok with that label, it kept me from bonding with people, it kept me safe. I had been hurt enough and was not about to allow anyone else to hurt me.

I had no idea how many hurt people there were in the world. Many people I have come in contact with have similar stories. I was ashamed of my past trauma and I thought people's knowledge of it would make them treat me differently. I also had no idea of how my issues with anger and depression were directly connected to my past. I simply thought I was crazy and was determined to keep my craziness a secret from the world.

When I was finally able to open up and begin to share my story with others, I realized that there were so many others in the world that have endured tragic circumstances. There were many abandoned children. There were many people living with un-diagnosed PTSD (Post-traumatic Stress Disorder). I realized that I was not alone, and that I wasn't crazy after all.

There are so many people in this world who have been hurt and abused and they are attempting to keep it together, never seeking the help needed to fully heal from their past, or even realizing that help exists. This is why sharing the tools that helped me with the readers of this book is so important to me.

I did not attempt to attack my issues until much later in life. I pray that by sharing my mental and emotional transformation tools with others, it won't take that long for another person to get the help they need, and they can begin living a happy, healthy life sooner than I did.

As I mentioned earlier, unfavorable life experiences have caused humans to develop what I describe as "Holes." We all have them in some form. These holes are formed from past unresolved pain and trauma. I personally walked around with huge holes in my heart for many years, and as time past on I began to realize many people were existing in life with these same holes, some even larger than mine.

If these holes are left untreated, they grow larger and deeper. Our lives continue to move forward and sometimes we go on living not realizing that these wounds are even there. We neglect to recognize that these scars have not only affected our lives, but the lives of everyone around us. They prevent us from giving and receiving love the way God intended for it to be. We were born to love naturally, wholeheartedly and without fear, but when we have been denied love from the beginning of our lives holes form in our hearts.

I personally believe that small pieces of our soul escape through those holes and we spend our entire lives trying to retrieve them and piece ourselves back together again. We try to mend our holes and our wounds with other people. Unfortunately during this process of trying to heal, we hurt other people, sometimes unintentionally. We can be completely oblivious to the pain we are causing others. There were times when I had no idea why I reacted so explosively to certain situations. My friends and family had no idea either. They just chalked it up to me being a crazy hot head.

One day my ex husband Cody made a harmless, casual comment about liking the way a particular pair of shoes looked on a woman we saw in passing at the mall. I know he meant no harm whatsoever, but due to the holes in my heart, I interpreted his comment as if he was saying he wished I looked like her. In my mind, this meant he thought I wasn't good enough for him. We had such a secure relationship, he didn't think there would be any problem with commenting on another woman's shoes, and there shouldn't have been. Under normal circumstances there would not have been, but my holes were still untreated so you can imagine how I reacted; I exploded! Later that day, I went into the house and took every single pair of shoes that i owned and threw them at his head, screaming, *"Since you like her shoes so much and you don't like mine then here you go!"* He and I laugh about this today, but but it wasn't funny then.

Since my mother didn't love me, I was afraid that no one ever would. I had people in my life that clearly loved and cared about me, I had not yet learned to completely love myself, and would never be able to love him and accept love from him until I closed my holes.

Since I took the time to dissect my issues, I have grown so much. That growth started with identifying what my triggers were and why they existed. I had to dig deep into my past and connect the dots. Doing that work can be painful, but in the end, it will allow you to live a better quality of life.

Another example of how my "Holes" affected my personal relationships was when I was eighteen years old, less than a year after my grandmothers murder. My older sister had gone off to University of California, San Diego to attend college. I was living with my Aunt SaBra whom i was named after, my father's only sister and the only daughter to the grandmother that raised me. After my grandmother's funeral, I was still in the my aunt took on the responsibility of raising me. She owned a four-unit apartment building on 94th and Normandie. She moved me in with her. My father's older brother Charles Fisher also lived on the property.

We didn't have a lot of family left and I was still in a very fragile state. My sister Mary called home from college to say she would not be coming home for Thanksgiving and Christmas. Now this is actually a normal thing for a new college student. She was adjusting to her new life, and aside from being a student she had gotten a new job, but because of the untreated "holes" in my heart, I was devastated by the fact that my only sister was not coming home. I felt so alone, and although her decision had absolutely nothing to do with me, I wasn't emotionally strong enough to view it any other way than yet another abandonment.

All I knew was I needed my sister, I missed her, she was all I had. I cried so hard because she couldn't come, I ranted and raved. I wasn't emotionally secure enough to understand that she simply had work and school and it wasn't convenient for her to return to Los Angeles at that time. She was also still grieving from the loss of our beloved grandmother whom we had just buried in May.

I reacted the way I did because I had severe abandonment issues and fear of loss. Our father died when I was ten. Our mother was still heavily addicted to drugs and absent from our lives. We lost the only consistent person in our lives that loved us. We were instantly snatched out of the home we grew up in and our lives were never the same.

The cause of my irrational behavior was much deeper than I could understand, but it would be years before I would even scratch the surface of the root psychological causes.

Once I did, I came to accept that because I had been abandoned, I did not feel valuable.

Nothing actually changes in our lives until we recognize and acknowledge our wounds and actually begin to deal with them. Physical scrapes and scratches will begin the natural healing process on their own; nature heals them in a few days with or without our help. Mental and emotional scars on the other hand, the ones we can't see require conscious action from us to get better.

Whatever method is needed for you to work on closing your holes, I urge you to identify and utilize it. Doing so will enhance the quality of your life. It will bring you a certain level of peace that many victims of abuse don't believe they will ever experience.

For me, forgiveness was a key part of filling in my holes. I needed to forgive my mother for abandoning me. Once I started to work on that, the gigantic gaping hole that I had gotten so used to camouflaging began to close.

Some of you have been trying very hard to heal without acknowledging what happened to you. You have been trying to move forward while pretending you were not affected. You have been trying to forgive while you are still bleeding. You have been trying to be okay for everyone else while your inner child is still waiting to be comforted. The truth is, you cannot heal what you will not name. Giving a name to the pain is not making it larger. It is giving it a place to go. It is giving it language and direction. It is bringing it out of your body and into the light where it can finally be processed and healed.

There is also a spiritual side to this. Because trauma can distort the way you see God. If you were hurt by someone who was supposed to protect you, you may struggle to trust God's protection. If you were abandoned, you may struggle to believe God stays. Being judged harshly, may cause you to struggle to believe God is gentle and kind. If you were controlled, you may struggle to surrender. Trauma can cause you to be afraid. You may love God, but still expect punishment. You may pray, but still feel undeserving. You may believe in blessings, but still feel like you are the exception. That is why healing the root is not just emotional, it is spiritual. God is not asking you to carry distorted beliefs about Him. He wants to heal the way you see Him too.

Finding the root also means noticing your patterns without shaming yourself. Every pattern has an origin story. The way you cope did not come out of nowhere. The way you shut down was learned. The way you stay busy was learned. The way you avoid conflict was learned. The way you pick the wrong people over and over was learned. The way you over give and allow others to take advantage of you was learned. The way you keep quiet when you should speak up, was a learned behavior. Patterns are protection strategies that became habits. They were created when you needed them. But what protected you then may be poisoning you now. And you do not have to hate yourself for that. You just have to be honest enough to change.

It takes courage to go to the root because roots are hidden. They are where you buried things you were not ready to feel. Let me tell you what happens when you heal the root. You stop reacting like you are still in the past. You stop living as if the worst thing is always about to happen again. You no longer give your power to old memories. You stop interpreting every moment through old pain. You start responding from the present moment. You accept that you can indeed be happy and you begin designing the life you desire.

Here is the part I need you to hear with your whole spirit. Finding the root is not meant to break you down. It is meant to free you. It is meant to show you what you have been carrying. It is meant to release shame and embrace self love. Shame tells us that something is wrong with us. The truth changes the conversation you have with yourself, and the conversation you have with yourself changes your life.

You deserve to heal deeply and permanently, not just temporarily. You deserve to stop treating depression like a mysterious fog that engulfed you, and start understanding the story behind it. It is time to stop blaming yourself for the way your body and mind respond when they have been through too much.

Show yourself patience and love. Find the root and pull it up gently, with compassion, with support, with prayer, and with love.

Because you are not just trying to feel better. You are trying to live a better life. You are trying to breathe again and become spiritually whole. Please believe me when I tell you that, it is possible. Peace of Mind, Happiness, Prosperity and Self-Love is possible for us all.

5

Open Your Curtains

Depression can make your bed feel like the safest place in the world and the most suffocating place at the same time. A Dark room with the curtains closed becomes your safe space. It becomes a hiding place, a shelter, a pause button, and sometimes a prison. The world outside the covers feels too loud, too demanding, too heavy. Your mind starts listing everything you have to do, everything you didn't do, everything you should have done, everything you don't have the energy to face. Before your feet even touch the floor, you feel defeated. Not because you're lazy or you do not care, but because your soul is tired. That kind of exhaustion is deeper than sleep. It is emotional. This kind of tired is the kind that makes you wonder if you will ever feel like yourself again.

If you are in that place, I need you to listen to me carefully. Getting out of bed is not a small thing when you are depressed. It is a victory. It is a battle that you have won. Getting up is proof that there is still some fight left in you, even if you feel differently.

People who have never experienced depression may not understand why it's hard to do what others do so simply. But you are not useless or lazy. You are not making excuses, or over-reacting. You are dealing with an invisible enemy that changes how your mind and body feels. Still reading this book. Still filled with hope. Still searching for a way back to light. That matters. You matter, and never let anyone or any situation make you feel like you don't.

Depression often tries to convince you that if you can't do everything, you should do nothing. It speaks in extremes. It makes you believe that unless you have the energy to tackle your whole life, it's pointless to do anything at all. But healing doesn't happen through extremes. Healing happens through small wins. Quiet wins. Unseen wins. Wins that look like nothing to other people but feel like everything to you. A small win is not a consolation prize. It is the foundation. It is how you build momentum when you have none. It is how you return to yourself one breath at a time. Applaud yourself for the small wins. You will have larger ones soon.

Sometimes the first small win is opening your eyes and not immediately judging yourself for being alive. Sometimes the first win is sitting up. Opening the curtains and allowing the sun to come int. Sometimes it's swinging your legs over the side of the bed. Sometimes it's putting your feet on the floor and whispering, I'm going to try. Sometimes it's drinking water. Sometimes it's washing your face. Sometimes it's making your bed not because you feel amazing, but because you want to change the energy in the room. Sometimes it's stepping outside for two minutes and letting the air touch your skin. Sometimes it's answering one text. Sometimes it's eating something small. Sometimes it's taking your medicine or calling your therapist.

Sometimes it's praying one honest sentence. Small wins are sacred because they are acts of self-respect when you feel like you have none.

You have to change the way you measure progress. Depression makes you compare yourself to who you were on your best day. It makes you compare yourself to people who aren't fighting the same battle. It makes you feel like you're failing because you can't keep up. But your progress is not measured by perfection. Your progress is measured by return. By the fact that you keep coming back. You keep trying again. You keep choosing life again. You keep choosing a next step again. That is strength. That is resilience. That is victory.

There is something spiritual about small wins because they require humility. They require you to accept that you are in a season where you must take your time. They urge you to stop rushing the process. They encourage you to stop shaming yourself for not being "back to normal" yet. Sometimes depression is the season where God teaches you how to be gentle with yourself. How to listen to your body and rest without guilt. How to stop performing. How to stop pretending you can carry everything and everybody. You matter most. Sometimes healing begins when you finally admit, I need help, and you stop arguing with your own needs. The burden of depression is too big to carry alone. Even if it's just one person. Reach out to them.

Eventually you will rebuild trust with yourself and the world around you. Depression breaks that trust. It makes you doubt your ability to follow through. It makes you feel unreliable to yourself. You make plans and then you cancel them. You promise yourself you'll do something and you don't. You start believing you can't even count on yourself. That belief can be crushing. Don't believe the lies. This too shall pass. Every small win is a deposit. Every time you do one tiny thing, you are telling yourself, I can trust me again. I am still here. I am still trying. I am still capable. You are rebuilding a relationship with yourself, and that relationship is part of your recovery. You have to become your biggest cheerleader.

If you are going to get out of bed again, you have to stop waiting for motivation to arrive like a visitor. Motivation often doesn't show up first. Movement shows up first. Action shows up first. The smallest action creates a spark, and the spark creates a little momentum. Depression makes you think you must feel better before you move, but sometimes you must move before you feel better. That movement can be tiny. It can be slow. It can be shaky. It can be imperfect. It still counts. Command yourself to get up and claim with your words that "Today is a Great day." Keep saying it and eventually it will be true.

Now let's talk about the shame that comes when you're in this kind of season. Shame will try to make you hide. Shame will try to make you isolate yourself from others. It will tell you that you should be embarrassed for struggling. It will tell you that other people can handle life, so why can't you. But shame is not your friend. It does not motivate you. On the contrary in will completely drain. Shame keeps you stuck in the bed because it makes you feel like you don't deserve to get up. The truth is, you deserve love and compassion. You deserve support. You deserve patience. You deserve to heal without being cruel to yourself. If no one is around to give you the love and compassion you need, you absolutely must give it to yourself.

Some days, getting out of bed again will require you to let

go of the idea that you must do it alone. You may need a safe person who checks on you. You may need a counselor who helps you understand your patterns. You may need a doctor to help you regulate what depression has disrupted. You may need a routine that is designed for your nervous system, not for somebody else's. You may need to simplify your life until you can breathe. That is not failure. That is wisdom. That is the kind of strength that chooses survival and recovery over pride. It is wonderful if you do have these supportive people in your life. But I don't want you to be lost when they leave. you are the prize in your world. Forming dependencies on other human beings can create a deeper problem. In this book i want you to learn the importance of bringing yourself out of those dark places.

I also want to speak to the part of you that feels like your life has been on pause. Depression can make you feel like you are losing time. Like you are getting older and falling behind. Like everyone else is moving forward and you're stuck in a slow-motion version of yourself. But hear me clearly, Please!. Rest is not wasted time when your soul is rebuilding. Healing is not delay. Healing is preparation. Healing is restoration. Healing is you becoming strong in a new way. Not strong for the world, but strong for you. If there is a day when you just can not get up. Lay there and listen to a uplifting YouTube video. Try Les Brown, Zig Ziglar, Wayne Dyer, Sadhguru, Shi Heng Yi, Maya Angelou, Tim Robbins, Joyce Meyers, Eric Et Thomas.

Small wins save you because they prove that hope can exist in small doses. You don't need to feel a sudden wave of joy to be healing. You don't need to wake up one day completely free to be progressing. You need a little light. A small smile at yourself in the bathroom mirror. A deep long breath. A little movement at a time. A little love and support. And you repeat those little things until they become a path.

One day, you will look back and realize your comeback was not one dramatic moment. It was a collection of small wins that nobody saw. The days you got up even though you didn't want to. The moments you chose to eat even though you had no appetite. The times you stepped outside even though you wanted to disappear. The prayers you whispered when you didn't have big faith. The boundaries you set when you were tired of being drained. The phone calls you finally made. The tears you finally let fall. The truth you finally told. Those were your turning points.

So if today all you can do is sit up in bed, that is enough. If all you can do is take a breath and say, I'm trying, let that be enough. You are healing, and healing takes spiritual internal work.

6

Getting Through the Day

Getting through the day can feel like carrying an invisible weight that never lets up. Depression has a way of pulling you downward without warning. A single thought turns into a flood. One memory opens the door to a whole hallway of regret. A rough moment early in the day convinces your mind that the rest of it is already ruined. Someone disappoints you, and suddenly that quiet voice starts whispering that nothing ever changes. The cycle of self sabotage begins.

Before you know it, you're not just sad, you're overwhelmed. Not just tired, you feel completely hopeless. Your thoughts begin replaying every mistake you have ever made, every bad choice, every "what if," and you find yourself questioning your entire life. That is how depression takes over and it tries to pass every painful thought off as truth. You can call it dark energy, negativity, or even the devil, but recognizing when it has grabbed hold of you is the first real step toward loosening its grip on your mind.

Here's what I want you to understand, gently and honestly: Depression is a mental and emotional loop that feeds on fear and exhaustion. It is a old repeated pattern, but it can be interrupted. No matter how familiar that cycle feels, it is not permanent. No matter how far down your thoughts have taken you, there is still a way back up. As long as you are have breath in your body, there is room for a reset, even if it has to happen one small moment at a time.

Hard days are going to show up, I can never promise you that they will never come again. That's not negativity, that's life. Healing doesn't mean every day will feel light and easy. It means teaching yourself how to respond when the heaviness arrives. Gathering up the strength to get out of bed, no matter what. It means refusing to let one difficult moment define who you are. Taking notice when your thoughts start running wild and making a choice to stop the mind chatter, even if it feels uncomfortable. Taking your power back doesn't always look calm or graceful. Sometimes it happens with shaky hands and a tired heart. But each time you do it, even in the smallest way, you prove to yourself that depression does not get to run your day

I describe it as going from mental and emotional poverty to power. That power is inside of all of us. We all possess the ability to influence our thoughts and emotions. You simply, first, have to believe that you are in control, and secondly, you must learn the tools to activate the power inside of you.

Let me be clear: this is not about religion. So it does not matter if you call that power God, Universe, Yahweh, Ala, Ra, Chi, Divine Consciousness or Prana. Every human being, no matter what religion they are, has this amazing power within them. Every human being has unseen energy moving through them, and it is capable of working in their favor.

No one group of people is more deserving of blessings and

love. We are all the same in worth, no matter what our belief system is. I use the word God in this book because that is my belief, but everyone is worthy and entitled to the same joy, the same good health, and the same prosperity, no matter what race, gender, economic status, or religion they are. I do not want you for one minute to think that if you have different beliefs, Or because you use a different word to describe the Divine Source that you are now stuck in the spiral of depression with no help. You are not. You are a powerful being with limitless potential. Do not allow society, or anyone, to make you believe you deserve less because you believe differently. We can all have a great life. We can all rise and be happy and successful. We can all live up to our fullest potential. The most significant belief you need to ensure a great quality of life is your belief in yourself. Believe that you are worthy of everything this amazing world has to offer, No Matter What!

One of the first reasons depression grabs you strongly at times is because you treat the thoughts you have during them like the are facts. Depression doesn't just drop a thought, it drops a conclusion. It says, "You're not enough," and you accept it. It says, "Nobody cares," and you accept it. It says, "You'll always be like this," and you accept it. And the moment you accept it, your body responds like it's true. Your shoulders tighten. Your chest gets heavy. Your appetite shifts. Your energy crashes. Your entire energetic vibration lowers and your uncontrolled emotions flood in. That is why the spiral feels physical, because your body is reacting to a story.

This chapter is about changing the story before it takes over the room, before it takes over your life. Sometimes stopping the spiral begins with something that sounds almost too simple. You simply pause and take a deep breath. You identify what's happening int that moment. You stop calling it your personality and you start calling it what it is. You say, "This is a spiral." You say, "This is depression talking." You say, "My nervous system is activated." You say, "I am triggered right now." Naming it is not weakness. Naming it is acknowledging it. You cannot fight what you won't identify. You cannot heal what you wont admit is happening. That one of the first steps.

I used to describe depression as a tennis ball traveling quickly at my head. As I began to heal, I realized that I was holding the tennis racket. I imagined taking a firm stance, racket in hand and swatting that tennis ball far away with everything in me. This worked for me. Create a visual for yourself of winning the war with depression and use that visual when you feel it coming on.

When you are in a hard moment, your mind wants to time travel. It wants to drag you into the past and punish you with memories. Or it wants to drag you into the future and terrify you with "what if." The spiral feeds on time travel. It gets stronger when you leave the present. So one of the most powerful things you can do is come back to right now. Not tomorrow. Not last year. Not five minutes from now. Right now. Bring yourself right back into the present moment. Begin to tell yourself that you are safe in this moment. You are breathing in this moment. You are still here in this moment. And that is enough to build from.

This is where spirituality becomes more than a concept. This is where God becomes more than a belief. Because in the hard moments, you need something steady, something higher than your feelings and stronger than the lie. Depression will try to make you believe you are alone, but you are not alone. Even if you feel lonely, you are not abandoned. Even if you feel far from

God, He is not far from you. Feelings shift, but God remains the same always. The spiral is loud, but it has no authority over a strong, confident mind anchored in truth.

And here is what makes that truth so powerful: faith is not pretending you don't hurt, it's refusing to let hurt become your identity. It's being able to say, "This is heavy," without also saying, "This is hopeless." It's learning how to sit in the storm without surrendering to it. Your emotions may feel real in the moment, but they are not the final verdict on your life. Just like all things, there is a season, and it will pass. The darkness may visit, but it does not get to move in. The feelings may rise, but they do not get to rule. When you hold onto God in the hard moments, through prayer, through breath, through one honest sentence at a time, you are building spiritual stability, and stability is what carries you until the light shows up again.

Hard moments can make you speak against yourself. That's another way the spiral wins. You start labeling yourself. You start saying, "I'm stupid." "I'm broken." "I'm a mess." "I can't do anything right." And every word you speak becomes a weight you carry. So in the hard moments, your mouth matters. Not because you're pretending, but because you're fighting for your life. Your mouth can either feed the spiral or starve it. Your mouth can either keep you trapped or help you climb. You don't need fancy words. You need strong words. You need words that hold you up. Words like, "I am having a hard moment, but I will make it through." or "Today is difficult but tomorrow will be better." Words like, "This is heavy, but it is temporary." Words like, "I have survived worse than this." Words like, "I am not quitting on myself today." or "I'm getting better and better everyday."

Sometimes stopping the spiral means choosing one simple

action that returns you to your body. Depression can pull you into your head so deeply that you forget you have a body that can help you regulate. Your body can become your anchor. Your breath can become your rope. Your senses can become your ladder. When the spiral is trying to pull you under, coming back into your body can save you. Even small things can become healing tools. Water on your face. Sunlight on your skin. Sitting upright. Opening a window. Stepping outside. Planting your bare feet in the grass. Putting your hand on your chest and reminding yourself, "I am here." These are not random tricks. These are ways of signaling safety to your system. The spiral cannot thrive as easily when your body is grounded.

Hard moments also expose what you need. Sometimes the spiral is a sign that you're depleted. Just like the body shows clear danger signs when you are depleted of water. The mind is the same way.

Sometimes the onset of depression is not even about a specific situation. Physical exhaustion can bring it on. Sometimes you've been giving too much of yourself to others and receiving too little in return. Sometimes you've been trying to be strong while ignoring your own needs. Depression loves depletion because depletion weakens your resistance. That's why taking care of your basic needs is not "selfish," it's warfare. It's protection. It's how you stay in the fight.

You also have to be careful about isolation during hard moments. Depression will tell you to disappear, to stop answering, to cancel everything, to retreat into silence. And sometimes you do need quiet. Sometimes you do need rest. But there is a difference between resting and hiding. The spiral gets stronger when you are alone with your darkest thoughts for too long. If you have one safe person, one prayer partner, one therapist, one friend who understands, hard moments are the time to reach out. Not when you feel strong enough, but when you feel tempted to spiral deeper. You do not have to carry the hard moments by yourself.

I want you to understand something important. Stopping the spiral does not always look like suddenly feeling better. Be patient with yourself. Sometimes stopping the spiral looks like choosing not to go further down. It looks like preventing a bad hour from becoming a bad day. It looks like getting through the moment without harming yourself, without numbing yourself, without abandoning yourself. It looks like saying, "I'm not okay, but I'm still here." That is victory. That is progress. That is a tool working.

Now you are learning how to lead yourself through darkness. You are developing the skills to comfort yourself when you are down. You are learning how to pause instead of panic. In this book you learn how to interrupt the lie before it becomes your whole mood. It will teach you to recognize the warning signs and respond with care instead of shame. That is what mature healing looks like. It's not dramatic. It's consistent. It's brave. It's daily. But it is possible.

Let me say this with love. If your hard moments ever include thoughts of harming yourself, you deserve immediate support. You deserve someone to talk to right away. Not because you're weak, but because your life is precious. If you ever feel like you are in danger, call your local emergency number or reach out to a crisis hotline in your area. In the United States, you can call or text 988 for the Suicide and Crisis Lifeline. You don't have to explain everything perfectly. You just have to reach. Help is not something you earn. Help is something you deserve.

You are not meant to fight alone or spiral in silence. You do not have to carry the weight without support. You are meant to heal and live a happy, prosperous life. You are meant to rise up like a phoenix from everything that you have been through and feel light, happy and free again. The hard moments are real, but they are not the end of your story. They are simply moment that you are now learning how to move through without letting them steal your future.

One significant tool that worked for me when I was depressed was a book by Michael Singer called the "Untethered Soul." it was my first introduction to the fact that we have a little voice in our head, a internal voice that is not always guiding us correctly.

The internal voice is a product of your subconscious mind. It is fueled by your fears and doubts until you learn to reprogram it. In this book I offer techniques that will assist you in reprogramming and officially declaring war on that negative voice in your head.

Declaring war and effectively winning that war with the enemy of the mind should be the ultimate goal. If the war is won with-in, all external enemies won't even have the ability to affect us. The true battle is in the mind. Gaining the abilities to control our thinking patterns. Learning to master control of our thoughts will allow us the privilege of only accepting thoughts that serve us well to enter into our mind space and we will develop the ability to cast out negative thoughts and images because they are the true internal enemy.

Maintaining a persistent negative thinking pattern will prove to be more harmful to you than anything you can ever encounter in your life. We must learn the tools needed to declare all out war on anything that prevents us from leading a happy fulfilling life. This is one of the main reasons why I felt compelled to write this book. It is my desire to share with the world the tools that helped me change my negative mindset. Developing these tools are the reason I will never be depressed again. This is my prayer for you as well.

The first step in changing self-deprecating internal dialogue is identifying it. Pay attention to what the enemy of your mind has been saying to you on repeat. Notice the thoughts that show up when you're tired, overwhelmed, or alone. Ask yourself what that inner voice has convinced you of that simply is not true. Once you can name the lie, it loses some of its power. You don't have to fight every thought, but you do need to stop agreeing with the ones that hurt you. That awareness is how you start getting through the day without letting depression run it.

7

Listen to Your Body

Depression is not only a battle in your mind. It lives in your body too. It changes your energy. It changes your appetite and your sleep. It zaps you of all motivation. It causes you to feel heavy and unattractive. It takes over as soon as you wake up. When you are depressed you become easily irritated. The smallest things frustrate you and cause you to shut down. It makes you want to isolate yourself from the rest of the world.

It makes you feel like a worthless failure. But you are not. Do not believe any of that, although I know from experience that it does feel real. I wish I could prove to you that you will feel better with each passing day and eventually depression will never knock on your door again.

Your body is always communicating. It talks through fatigue and tension. It talks to you through headaches and stomach issues. It talks through restlessness. It talks through craving a unnecessary amount of food. It talks through numbness. It talks through that feeling of being "off" even when you cannot explain it. Depression can make you feel like your emotions have no logic or reason, but often your body is carrying the reason.

Sometimes your mind is not being dramatic. Sometimes your body is unbalanced. The most powerful thing you can do is stop judging yourself and start listening.

Sleep is one of the first places depression shows up. Either you cannot sleep, or you sleep too much, and even after a full night you still feel tired. Depression can make your mind race at night and crash during the day. It can make your body feel heavy like it is filled with sand. It can make you dread the night because the quiet time gives your thoughts room to get loud. When your sleep gets disrupted, your mood gets more fragile. Everything feels harder when you are tired. Your patience gets shorter. Your confidence gets lower. Your emotions become quicker to flood. It becomes easier to spiral. That is not weakness. That is biology. Your brain cannot regulate well without rest.

But here is the part that gives you power. You do not have to fix your entire sleep life overnight to start healing. You just need to treat sleep like it matters. Because it does. Try to develop a feeling of gratitude for sleep. Depression will tell you to stay up scrolling, to stay in your head, to stay wired, to stay distracted, to avoid quiet. But your healing requires rest. Not just physical rest, but nervous system rest. Sometimes the most spiritual thing you can do is create a softer night. A calmer, peaceful routine. A bedtime that honors your mind and body instead of punishing them. Rest is not laziness. Rest is repair. Your body is replenishing itself. Find positive affirmations on YouTube and listen to them while you are attempting to fall asleep. This was a tool that worked wonders for me.

A lot of people over eat when they are down and others lose their appetite completely. The ones who eat constantly, it is not because they are hungry, but because they are trying to soothe something. Depression can make you crave sugar, carbs, and comfort foods, because your body is searching for quick relief. And then shame shows up. You judge yourself for eating too much or eating too little. But shame does not heal the body. Shame weakens it. Your body needs nourishment to fight. Your brain needs fuel to regulate. When you are depressed, eating can feel like work, but every time you nourish yourself, you are telling your system, I care about you. You are telling your body, We are not giving up.

Movement is one of the most misunderstood parts of depression recovery. People hear "exercise helps" and it can feel insulting when you can barely get out of bed. But movement does not have to mean a gym, a workout plan, or a perfect routine. Movement is simply telling your body, we are still alive. It can be stretching in your bed. It can be walking to the mailbox. It can be standing in the sunlight for a few minutes. It can be dancing in your kitchen for one song. Sometimes its slow small movements. But movement changes chemistry. Movement moves stuck energy. It helps your nervous system discharge what it has been holding. Depression often makes your body freeze, and gentle movement helps you thaw out.

Mood is not only emotional. Mood is physical too. Your hormones and stress levels matter. Your blood sugar matters. How much water you drink makes a difference because hydration is vital. Your vitamins matter. Adequate sunlight makes a huge difference in your mood. Your nervous system matters. That is why you can wake up and feel heavy for no obvious reason. That is why your mood can drop after days of poor sleep. That is why you can feel anxious when you have not eaten. You feel irritable when you are dehydrated. Sometimes the enemy is not your character and your mood may not be the result of a situation. Sometimes the enemy is your body needing care.

This chapter is not here to make you feel like you need to become perfect to heal. It is here to remind you that healing is possible. Each day you get up is progress. You are not a floating spirit separated from your body. You are one system. And your system deserves patience and compassion. When you begin caring for your body, you are not being shallow. You are being wise by giving yourself a stronger foundation to do the emotional work. You are making the battle easier by strengthening the vessel you live in.

Spiritually, this matters because your body is not an afterthought. Your body is sacred. Your body has carried you through things you do not even talk about. It has survived heartbreak. It has survived trauma. Your body has survived disappointment, grief, and stress. It has still shown up for you even when you did not know how to show up for yourself. So when depression tries to make you hate your body, neglect your body, punish your body, ignore your body, you have to remember that your body is not your enemy. Your body is your partner in healing. It is the beautiful vessel that houses your infinite spirit.

Sometimes the most powerful prayer is not just asking God to remove depression. Sometimes the prayer is asking God to teach you how to care for yourself. How to slow down and gain control of your thoughts. How to rest without guilt. How to eat with love. How to move with gentleness. How to listen. How to notice what your body is saying before it has to scream. Because your body will eventually scream if it is ignored long enough. Many people call it depression when it is actually years of unprocessed stress living in the body.

Take care of yourself. You are allowed to rebuild your

life through care and self-love. You can create a routine that supports your healing. You can take your mental health seriously You are allowed to treat your body like it deserves to be here. Because it does.

I need you to understand this. Caring for your body is not separate from your healing journey. It is part of the journey. The more you honor your body, the more your mood has a chance to stabilize. The more stable your mood becomes, the more clearly you can think, and controlling how you think is detrimental to your healing. When your thoughts are clear the easier it becomes to break the thought cycle. The easier it becomes to stop the spiral. The easier it becomes to face triggers with wisdom. Your body and your mind are connected, and when you support one, you support the other.

So if all you can do today is sit up and take a sip of water and lay back down, let that be a win. If all you can do is eat a small bite of something, let that be a win. If you are able to take a short walk to the end of the driveway and feel the sun on your face, that's definitely a win. Your healing is not measured by large leaps. It is measured by consistent love and care. It is measured by showing up for yourself in small ways every day until the small ways become a new way of life.

8

Your Peace is Priceless

Depression is not always caused by what is inside you. Sometimes it is what keeps reaching you. Sometimes it is what keeps draining you. Quite often it is what keeps demanding more than you can give, and what keeps getting access to your head and your heart without permission. When you have been living without boundaries, your spirit becomes tired in a way that sleep cannot fix, because sleep restores the body, but boundaries restore the soul. And if you are serious about healing, you have to be serious about protecting your peace. I have had to set hard boundaries with many of my friends and family. I won't say the decision to do so is an easy one. However, it is vital when you are trying to save your own life.

A boundary is not a wall that keeps love out. A boundary is a door that lets you decide what comes in and what stays out. It is the difference between being kind and being used. It is the difference between being supportive and being drained. It is the difference between being generous and being depleted. Many people struggle with boundaries because they confuse them with being mean. They think boundaries make them selfish.

They think saying no makes them a bad person. They think putting themselves first makes them unloving. But the truth is, boundaries are not cruelty. Boundaries are clarity.

When I was still quite emotionally broken, I allow friends and family to use me. I paid for all the dinners and offered financial support to able-bodied adults who took me for granted. Because I was so desperate for love, I did it willingly. Once I healed that all stopped lol. Once you learn to love yourself, you notice that some people would not to the same for you if you needed them.

Depression often grows in people who are always giving and rarely receiving, people who are always showing up and rarely being poured into, people who are always listening and rarely being heard, people who carry everybody's emotions while their own emotions stay locked up. When you live like that, you can become emotionally bankrupt. Then you start blaming yourself for not having energy, not having joy, not having patience, not having motivation. But you cannot keep pouring from an empty cup. At some point, your mind and body will force you to stop. Sometimes depression is that force. It is your system saying, I cannot keep doing this.

Protecting your peace begins with telling the truth about what drains you, not what drains other people, not what "shouldn't" bother you, but what actually drains you. Certain conversations drain you. There are many people in your life that drain you. You can be drained by certain environments. Having expectations of others will drain you. You have been trying to incessantly pray for those draining people when you actually need to protect yourself from them. Prayer is indeed powerful, but prayer does not replace wisdom. Pray for them from a distance. Prayer does not replace boundaries and it does not replace the decision to stop letting chaos have constant access to you.

Some of you were taught that love means unlimited access. I definitely felt that way. We are raised to believe that family means you endure anything. That being a good friend means you always say yes. That being a good partner means you tolerate disrespect. That being spiritual means you never get upset. That being positive means you never set limits. These are the biggest lies we ever told ourselves. it a person offers nothing but drama and turmoil to your life, you must back away from them. Love without boundaries becomes resentment, and resentment is heavy. It sits in your chest. You find yourself-talking to yourself throughout the day, saying all the things you wish you would have said. Sticking up for yourself in your head because you did not have the courage to actually do it. That makes you tired and irritable. It makes you shut down. It makes you feel guilty for feeling what you feel. Eventually, it can deepen depression because you start feeling trapped in a life that does not honor you.

I have a sister whose adult behavior is disrespectful and toxic. I wanted to build a closer relationship with her because we were not raised together. However, every time she came around, she acted as if I owed her something, almost like she felt entitled and had the idea that I was financially responsible for her, and she was in her forties. I tolerated it for a while because she was my blood, but eventually I had to distance myself from her. I'm still open to a relationship, but I have done so much work to heal from all of my past trauma that I have little to no patience for her antics. I pray that changes one day, because I truly would love for us to enjoy a peaceful, sisterly relationship.

Boundaries are healing because they teach your nervous

system safety. When you have no boundaries, your body stays on edge. You never know when someone will call with drama, like the sister I described earlier. You never know when someone will need something. You never know when someone will demand your attention. You never know when someone will cross the line again. That unpredictability creates stress. Stress creates exhaustion. Exhaustion creates vulnerability. And depression loves vulnerability. When you set boundaries, your body relaxes and your mind quiets. Your spirit breathes easier and deeper, not because life becomes perfect, but because your life becomes protected.

There is also a spiritual reason boundaries matter. You cannot grow in environments that keep cutting you down. You cannot heal around people who keep reopening your wounds. You cannot hear God clearly when you are surrounded by noise, manipulation, and pressure. Boundaries are not just emotional decisions. They are spiritual alignment. Some people simply are not meant to be in your life. They are not part of your path. You must choose peace over performance. They are you choosing health over guilt. They are you choosing wisdom over fear. They are you trusting that God will still love you even when you say no.

One of the hardest parts about boundaries is accepting that some people will not like them. Many will say that you think you are better than them. People who benefited from your lack of boundaries will resist when you finally create them. People who are used to you over-giving will act like you changed. People who are used to you being available for them, will guilt you when you take a step back. The ones who are used to you saying yes will get uncomfortable when you say no. Depression will try to convince you that their discomfort means you are wrong. But their discomfort may simply mean they can no longer control you. Healing often requires disappointment, not your disappointment, but theirs. You will disappoint people when you stop abandoning yourself and put yourself first. That is a part of recovery. Do not be afraid to pour all the energy you have into yourself. It is what you need to have the strength to master *"Kicking Depression in the Butt"*

I have four amazing children, one son and three daughters, and I absolutely adore them. One key component I learned in maintaining positivity is putting myself first. Yes, I know most parents spend their entire lives putting their kids first. That is what we are taught to do. However, if you do not put yourself first, you are in no mental and emotional condition to give your children the best version of you.

When I was a younger parent, I thought my feelings and needs did not matter as long as the kids were happy. Most parents think this way. They believe they must sacrifice everything because they chose to be parents. That was definitely how I felt. Now I feel differently. There is so much work that needs to be done to live a happy, peaceful life. If you neglect yourself and only focus on making your children happy, you will look up and find yourself a senior citizen who is sad, depressed, and unfulfilled. Your children will have married and gone on with their own lives, checking in with you only on holidays, busy creating their world. Making sure your own emotional and mental needs are covered first is not selfish. Life goes on after parenthood. I now know how important it is to make sure I am happy as well.

Because of my past, I have grown up with many emotional deficiencies. I felt unwanted, and my self-esteem was very low. I became a parent long before I even attempted to seek healing from my past. Because I still carried so much past trauma, my love for my kids was what I considered unhealthy. I was a great parent by society's standards. I worked hard and provided everything they wanted and needed. I even tried to make sure I showed plenty of affection and attended to the best I knew how to all of their emotional needs. I encouraged and uplifted them, hugged and kissed them regularly, and I went to all their school functions and always showed up for them as a mother. As far as I was concerned, I was the best parent ever.

However, that didn't leave any time for me to attend to my own needs. Honestly, I can't say that in my early twenties and thirties, I even realized I had unattended emotional and mental needs. Although I knew I had been through trauma, I didn't know I could seek help from the recurring memories and pain. I didn't know many of my fears and reactions to certain situations were direct results of the trauma I had experienced. I didn't realize the obsessive way in which I loved my children was rooted in fear and trauma.

Protecting your peace also means recognizing that you are allowed to outgrow relationships. You are allowed to outgrow conversations. You can outgrow environments that keep you in survival mode. You can evolve from the version of you who tolerated everything. Stop negotiating with disrespect. Stop letting others hurt and abuse your kindness. No longer serve as someone's emotional punching bag. You are allowed to stop being the fixer of everyone else and solely concern yourself with fixing you. You are allowed to stop being the one who holds everyone together while you secretly fall apart inside. This is not about becoming cold. This is about becoming whole.

Sometimes the boundary is **external.** You stop answering late-night calls. You limit contact. You stop explaining yourself to people who twist your words. You stop going places that trigger you. You stop allowing certain conversations to continue. You stop giving your time to people who only call when they need something. You stop letting your phone become an emergency room for everybody else's emotions. These boundaries create space in your life, and space is where healing grows.

Sometimes the boundary is **internal.** You stop letting guilt make your decisions. You stop replaying what they said. You stop trying to prove your worth to yourself and others. You stop taking responsibility for other people's feelings. You stop blaming yourself for someone else's behavior. You stop negotiating your needs down to nothing. You stop abandoning yourself in order to be loved by others. Internal boundaries are powerful because they protect your peace even when life is loud.

When you start protecting your peace, you will notice something. Your energy returns in small waves. Your mind begins to clear. Your emotions become less intense. You start feeling more like you. You may even start hearing your own voice again, the voice you buried under everybody else's needs and expectations, the voice that knows what you need, the voice that knows what you can handle, the voice that knows when something is too much. Depression often mutes that voice. Boundaries bring it back.

When the healing process begins, you no longer view everything as an attack against you. Your perspective widens to accommodate the feelings and points of view of others. It is currently December 23, 2025 and I continued working on myself. I continued putting myself first. That is what I want for each of you.

Today, I have healed many of my wounds. I used to call them "holes," which we all have, some are larger than others. Today, at age fifty-six, many of the gigantic "holes" left from the hurt and abuse that I walked around with are closed. I know not that I'm worthy of love and happiness, no matter how my life began. But that healing didn't drop out of the sky. I had to seek it out. I had to desire to stop viewing the world as horrid and me as its victim. I had to choose to stop being angry that I didn't have a perfect childhood. I had to forgive my parents for succumbing to their substance addictions.

Most importantly, I had to gain control over my thoughts. I had to practice replacing negative thoughts with positive ones, repeatedly, until it became a habit. That is the dream I have for you all. I dream you get to the point where I am now. Where you boldly and confidently say : *"I will Never be depressed again."* Do not give up because it is possible for you too.

Switching out the negative with the positive must become second nature to you. Your mind is the magical tool needed to transform your earthly experience into a happy, fulfilling one. We all deserve and can achieve happiness. Become better for yourself and no one else. Live for you; let every day's mission be for you to feel happiness and peace in every moment. You are the captain of your soul and your fate lies in your own hands. When you don't feel great, learn the tools to analyze and process the emotions you are having, then release them and move forward.

As long as you are alive, there will always be something that has the potential to cause you pain. Small, daily negative situations at home and work can, if you allow them to, can chip away at your happiness and peace. Acknowledge your feelings in every moment, learn from them, and proceed through life with your new found tools. Customize your tools for your life. Create personal affirmations specifically for your needs and the areas you want to improve in.

Throughout your daily life, you will have to pull many of those tools out of the toolbox to navigate through life and stay positive. Some of the transformational work may seem repetitive and tedious, but don't give up. Repetition is necessary to reprogram the mind. Commit the positive tools to habit, and soon you will rejoice in the evidence that they work. I assure you, you will see positive changes in your life and mindset.

When you struggle your entire life with love, or the absence of love, you form many unhealthy attachments. These attachments can cause you great pain. Because of being abandoned by my biological mother, my need for love was greater than others. Even though my mother's choices were drug-induced and perhaps "she wasn't in her right mind," it didn't prevent me from growing up feeling unwanted and unloved. Love is our true nature, and we shouldn't have to fight for it. We shouldn't have to live in constant fear of not being loved, and even when someone loves us, we shouldn't be afraid of losing their love.

This type of love is unhealthy. However, many people experience love in this unhealthy way. Until we do the emotional repairs on ourselves that are needed to learn to love without fear and teach ourselves how to have positive, healthy relationships, unfortunately, these are the relationships we will build with others. It may very well feel like love, but it is not. Love is kind. Love doesn't hurt. Until we let go of the belief that we don't deserve to be loved, our relationships with our parents, siblings, children, and spouses will all suffer. Every human being deserves to be loved. It took many years for me to realize that the possessive way I loved my children was coming from a place of fear. We have a fear of losing them because our love for them is so strong that we cannot bear the thought of being without them. However, we are loving them while carrying the wounds from our past that have yet to be healed.

Once I began healing and truly began knowing that I was a valuable person, my love lost the desperate undertone. By the time my children were adults, I was so full of self-love and admiration that small things like regular phone calls and holiday visits were no longer vital necessities. I was no longer crippled if they didn't reach out and assure me of their love. I finally loved myself. Loving myself became my primary focus. I enjoyed being in my own company. If my kids were busy with their own lives and didn't check in as much as I would have liked, I wouldn't take it personally, and it didn't crush my soul like it once would have. I could detach from that unhealthy, needy, can't live without them type of behavior. It does not mean your love for them has diminished. It simply means your love for yourself takes precedence over everything. You realize you too are the prize. You are a worthy, valuable being that adds to the lives of others as much as they do to yours. Arriving at this point in my life felt wonderful. People who have taught us to put everyone else and their needs before our own have done us a disservice. We can't truly love others until we master loving ourselves.

Breaking attachments productively is done in peace and love. It doesn't mean you love people any less. It isn't a negative "I'm done with them" situation. It means you no longer need their attention and presence the way you need food, water, and air. Other people do not control your life and emotional stability. It means that when you and a loved one don't agree on something, you no longer worry about the relationship being damaged and never seeing them again. I used to be afraid to voice an opposing opinion to my family. When you have those fear-based attachments, you find yourself not truly being yourself for fear of losing them. You become very passive and in agreement with things you very well might not agree with. You are subconsciously afraid to stand up for yourself or oppose anything because you think they will not love you anymore if you do. Although I lived that way for years, this is not a healthy way to love. I do not agree with explosive behavior of any kind, but there is always a kind, loving way to express your opinion or viewpoint on things. Your voice matters.

It took years for me to realize I was creating unhealthy attachments to friends, family, and lovers. They all feel like actual loving relationships until you truly know the difference. This is your world. If life is a play, you have the starring role. You should give no one the power to destroy your image of yourself. Let's say you run into a person you don't even know who is downright cruel, and this person says something mean to you like, "You're fat," or, "You are ugly." It is challenging to comprehend how a person can be so cruel when we are embodiment's of pure love. In the world we inhabit, there are many people who are truly hurting within themselves. Unfortunately, they will lash out at others. You could end up being the person they spew their evil onto that particular day. You must detach from their experience. It has nothing to do with you. You can't take anything they say about you to heart—their opinion of you is not a fact. How you feel about yourself is what matters. If we are honest with ourselves, we have all said something unkind to another person. I don't point that out to judge you, but to show you that we can choose to be better. We can identify the behavior in ourselves and others. We cannot change others, but we can change ourselves. We've all felt and inflicted the pain of hurtful words. Only then can we learn the lessons needed to understand it's all a choice—a choice to be mean to another, a choice to speak harsh words out of your mouth. We choose how we allow others to treat us. It is also a choice to avoid letting someone else's mistreatment affect our spirit, no matter who—parents, siblings, employers, spouses. Do not allow anyone to mistreat you. Usually, when we allow this behavior, it is because we have not recognized our worth. Regardless of who you are, you are worthy and deserving of love, respect, and kindness.

Detaching and setting boundaries comes in many forms. After twenty-six years, I changed the name of the salon I owned for twenty-six years. My Braiding salon took great care of me for years, but it was time for me to detach from the name "Braids By SaBrina" a name I advertised and worked hard to make a household name in the Los Angeles community. My staff and I drove the streets of Los Angeles in my burgundy H2 Hummer, flooding businesses, shopping centers, and parking lots with "Braids By SaBrina" flyers for many years. The decision to change the name and no longer offer the service of braiding wasn't an easy one. However, at this time in my life, I was dealing with a medical scare. After a tonsillectomy surgery the Doctor found a tumor called a Glomus Tympanicum. I knew in order for me to maintain a positive mindset while this tumor was still living in my head, I had to remove all negativity from my life. Four months earlier I had been feeling the urge for change anyway. I had given twenty-six years to the community, offering excellent service and giving jobs to over 1700 women, and even a few men in the Los Angeles community. I trained them all to be professional braiders and taught them how to advertise and sustain a business of their own.

There were many difficulties in being a consistent salon owner and governing over so many young people. It taught me to be a leader and showed me I could accomplish anything I set my mind to. I will be honest: I ruled with a stern "SaBrina's way or no way" motto. At five feet, two inches tall, I needed to establish authority or be run over by my many employees. I gave my all to that business, and I have no regrets. I will always be known as the famous "Braid Queen." To create a life of good health and peace, I had to eliminate the stress caused by my employees, getting them to take pride in the business and dealing with challenging attitudes and disrespectful behavior. As the salon owner, I was held accountable for their tardiness and rude attitudes. I had to address any of their mistakes with the clients because, after all, the salon was named Braids By SaBrina. I was young and a full-time mother, raising kids and trying to develop the young women who worked for me into potential business owners. It wasn't easy.

Finding out about the tumor had the potential to send me backwards emotionally. I vowed to never be depressed again so I knew I had to rid myself of the few very stressful employees I had left and create a environment of healing and peace until my surgery to remove the tumor. I sat down and prayed about it and God basically said "It's time, It's a New Day!. So seven days later I politely let go of the last for braiders, I changed all of the salons signs and fliers to "A New Vision Dreadlock Studio" and I never looked back. I worked in my salon alone for three more years. I serviced one client at a time. I was able to create a space of peace which prevented me from panicking every time I felt the tumor beating in my head. Yes it somehow was connected to my hearts rhythm. On January 2,3 and 4 of

2025. Dr. Ikera Isiyama successfully removed the tumor with no complications.

Let me remind you of something that matters. You are not called to carry what is killing you. You do not have to stay connected to what is breaking you down. You must stop saying yes while your mental health suffers. Your peace is not optional. It is not a luxury. Your peace is a requirement for your healing. Protecting your peace is not selfish. It is responsible.

You can love people and still need space from them. It is possible to forgive people and still set limits and boundaries. You can be kind and still say no. Be spiritual and still protect yourself. You can be a good person and still choose yourself. Boundaries are healing because they teach you that your life matters too. In fact, it matters most. Take care of yourself first and learn to monitor your thoughts and control your emotions. Your future is at stake. When you finally start living like the extraordinary person that you are, depression begins to lose its grip because you are no longer living in constant depletion. Healing from depression is possible, please hang in there.

9

The Day You Realize You're Still Standing

If you made it to this chapter, that already tells me something important about you. It tells me you didn't give up. Even if you wanted to. You may have been tired of trying, but you hung in there. Even if some days all you could do was exist. You kept going anyway, and that matters more than you probably realize right now. I am proud of you and you definitely should be proud of yourself.

Depression has a way of making you forget how strong you are. It convinces you that the days you struggled somehow cancel out the days you survived. It lies and tells you that because you're still fighting, you must be losing. That's not how this works. Staying alive through something that tries to take you out from the inside is not weakness. It is endurance. It is courage, even when it doesn't feel brave. Life is truly beautiful and you deserve to experience the best of it.

I want you to understand something very clearly. Healing does not mean you wake up one morning and everything is fixed. It means you slowly start trusting yourself again. You learn how to talk to yourself differently. It means you stop abandoning yourself when things get hard. You begin showing up for your own life in small, quiet ways that don't always get applause, but they add up. You truly learn to love yourself from the inside out.

There will still be days when your energy feels low. There will still be moments when your mind tries to drag you back into old patterns. That does not erase the progress you've made. It just means you're human. What changes now is that you recognize what's happening. You take a minute to pause and breathe. You remind yourself that you've been here before and you made it through. That awareness is power and each times will get easier and easier.

You don't need to become someone else to be okay. You don't have to fix everything about yourself. There is no need to prove your worth to anyone. You are worthy and you always have been. The version of you reading this is already more than enough. The pain you've carried does not disqualify you from joy. Mistakes you've made do not define your future. The hard seasons did not come to ruin you. They helped you evolve. They shaped your mind in ways you may not fully see yet.

I know there were days you questioned whether life would ever feel good again. I remember those days. The times when getting out of bed felt pointless. Days when you smiled for others while silently breaking on the inside. But still, here you are. Still reading this book. Still breathing and seeking help. You are still willing to believe there might be something better ahead. That tells me hope is still alive in you, even if it's tired and quiet.

Please remember this when things feel heavy again. You are not alone, nor are you crazy. You are not a weak burden to others. You are someone who has been through a lot and is learning how to live again. That takes time. That takes patience. That takes compassion, especially for yourself.

I want you to keep choosing yourself everyday. Keep choosing rest when you need it. Be honest with yourself when you are struggling. Seek support instead of silence when you are depressed. The world needs you here more than you know. Your story matters. Your life matters. You matter.

On the days when you forget that, come back to this moment. Remember that depression is not the boss of you. It did not take your spirit. Nor has it devalued your worth. Your future is still very bright. You are still standing and your story is not over.

There is so much more life ahead of you. More laughter, love and peace. There will be more moments that remind you why fighting for your happiness is worth it. You don't have to rush toward them. Just keep moving forward one day at a time. This is a battle you can win, and you will.

About the Author

SaBrina Fisher Reece writes self-help books rooted in emotional healing, personal growth, and spiritual awareness. Her work blends lived experience with motivational insight, often exploring themes of balance, resilience, self-mastery, and the unseen forces that shape our thoughts and behaviors. Drawing from both practical reflection and metaphysical concepts, her writing encourages readers to develop greater self-awareness, reconnect with their inner strength, and create more intentional, aligned lives.

You can connect with me on:

🌐 https://in59secondspublishing.com

f https://www.facebook.com/BraidQueenSaBrinaReece

Also by SaBrina Fisher Reece

For more than twenty-six years, she built one of the most influential braiding salons and schools in Los Angeles, **Braids By SaBrina**, earning statewide recognition as *"The Braid Queen."* Her success was self-made, built through discipline, resilience, and vision, often without consistent support or validation from others.

Shaped by early abandonment, profound loss, and hard-earned self-trust, SaBrina's life journey led her to explore emotional healing, spiritual alignment, and self-mastery. Today, she is an author, speaker, and guide dedicated to helping others develop inner balance, confidence, and emotional strength.

She is the author of numerous self-help and transformational works, including *My Spiritual Smile, Your Mind Is Magic, Perfectly Positive, Spiritual Balance, Living Life on a Higher Frequency, Become Your Own Cheerleader, Kicking Depression in the Butt, Self Sabotage, How to Get Exactly What You Want From God*, When I Say "I Am"

PROFOUND

Ancient Wisdom That Changed My Life is a deeply reflective exploration of consciousness, belief, and the timeless truths that shape human experience.

Blending personal journey with ancient teachings, this book invites readers to question what they have been taught about power, faith, fear, and inner authority. Through travel, study, and lived experience, the author uncovers patterns that appear again and again across cultures, philosophies, and spiritual traditions, all pointing to the same realization: transformation begins within.

From sacred sites in Peru, Egypt, and Greece to the writings of mystics, philosophers, and modern thought leaders, *Profound* bridges ancient wisdom with modern life in a way that feels grounded, honest, and accessible. This is not a book of dogma or rigid instruction. It is an invitation to think more deeply, observe more clearly, and reconnect with the part of yourself that has always known there was more.

Written for the seeker, the lifelong learner, and anyone who has ever felt confined by inherited beliefs, *Profound* challenges the idea that truth must be complex, distant, or mediated through fear. Instead, it offers a calm, thoughtful perspective on personal responsibility, inner growth, and the quiet power of awareness.

This book does not ask you to abandon faith, values, or reverence. It asks you to expand your understanding.

If you have ever questioned why certain knowledge is rarely discussed, why ancient civilizations seemed to understand something we have forgotten, or why your inner world feels more powerful than you were taught to believe, *Profound* will resonate deeply.

This is a book meant to be felt as much as read. A companion for reflection. A doorway to deeper awareness. A reminder that wisdom has always been closer than we think.

Spiritual Balance:
Spiritual Balance: Aligning Mind, Body, and Energy in Everyday Life is a grounded, insightful guide for anyone seeking clarity, emotional stability, and deeper alignment in a fast-moving world.

In this book, SaBrina Fisher Reece explores the truth that many people sense but struggle to articulate: life becomes chaotic when our inner energies are out of balance. Drawing from spiritual principles, lived experience, and practical awareness, *Spiritual Balance* breaks down how the mind, body, and energetic self are deeply interconnected—and how neglecting one inevitably affects the others.

This book reframes common spiritual concepts in a way that is accessible, realistic, and applicable to everyday life. Readers will learn that masculine and feminine energies are not tied to gender, but are universal forces present within every person. When these energies are balanced, we experience greater peace, confidence, emotional regulation, and healthier relationships. When they are not, stress, confusion, and emotional exhaustion take over.

Rather than offering abstract philosophy, *Spiritual Balance* provides readers with a new way of understanding themselves. It encourages self-awareness, intentional living, and emotional responsibility without shame or perfectionism. Topics include emotional balance, energetic boundaries, spiritual awareness, self-worth, and the role of unseen forces in shaping our daily experiences.

This book is for readers who know there is more to life than what can be seen, measured, or explained logically—but who also want something practical, grounded, and honest. *Spiritual Balance* meets spirituality where real life happens: in relationships, work, healing, growth, and everyday decisions.

By aligning mind, body, and energy, readers are guided toward a more peaceful, empowered, and intentional way of living—one that honors both the human experience and the spiritual truth beneath it.

www.ingramcontent.com/pod-product-compliance
Lightning Source LLC
Chambersburg PA
CBHW072045040426
42447CB00012BB/3032